Vocabulary Workbook

MW00878113

Daily Routines, Community, School

Vocabulary words, find the correct sentence, find the correct picture, find the missing words, write a sentence

Great for older students!

Contact the author :
aworldoflanguagelearners@gmail.commay

Table of Contents

Instructions for Use

Newcomer English Language Learners (ELLs) benefit from multiple exposure to vocabulary. This workbook gives students practice listening to sentences, identifying pictures, words, and sentences, and writing sentences.

The workbook has three sections: daily routines, community, and school. Each section follows the same format.

Vocabulary Sheets- There are pictures and words for important vocabulary for each section. Read the words to students if they are not yet able to decode them independently.

Sentence Listening- Each vocabulary word has a sample sentence that uses the word in context. Read the sentence and have students listen and follow along.

Sentence Choose the correct picture- Students read or listen to each sentence and then choose the matching picture from a choice of two.

Sentences Choose the correct sentence- There are three sentences for each picture. Students choose the sentence that best describes the picture.

Find the Missing Words- Students use the word banks to fill in the missing words for each sentence that matches the pictures.

Sentence Writing- Students write a sentence for each picture.

Daily Routine

waking up

getting dressed

eating breakfast

working out

getting out of bed

brushing teeth

eating lunch

putting on pajamas

making the bed

brushing hair

eating a snack

going to bed

washing your face

stretching

eating dinner

sleeping

Daily Routine

Daily Routine Vocabulary

doing laundry	leaving	driving a car	riding a bike
watching T.V.	washing dishes	going shopping	reading
cleaning	getting undressed	at work	doing homework
taking a shower	taking a bath	making dinner	getting on the bus

Daily Routine

Listen to the Sentences

	He is eating breakfast.
	He is brushing his teeth.
	She is working out.
	He is sleeping.
	He is reading a book.
	He is doing his homework.

Listen to the Sentences

She is watching T.V.

He is going to bed.

She is eating lunch.

She is brushing her hair.

He is getting dressed.

He is washing his face.

Listen to the Sentences

	He is doing laundry.
	He is brushing his hair.
	She is cleaning the house.
	She is getting out of bed.
	He is getting undressed.
	He is eating dinner.

Listen to the Sentences

	He is driving his car.
	He is at work.
	She is shopping for food.
	She is washing dishes.
	She is waking up.
	She is leaving the house.

Listen to the Sentences

	She is having a snack.
	She is stretching.
	She is making dinner.
	He is taking a bath.
	She is doing her homework.
	He is riding his bike.

Circle the picture that matches the sentence.

He is eating breakfast.	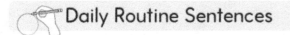	
He is brushing his teeth.		
She is working out.		
He is sleeping.		
He is reading a book.		
He is doing his homework.		

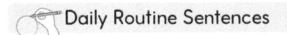

Circle the picture that matches the sentence.

She is watching T.V.		
He is going to bed.		
She is eating lunch.		
She is brushing her hair.		
He is getting dressed.		
He is washing his face.		

 Daily Routine Sentences

Circle the picture that matches the sentence.

He is doing laundry.		
He is brushing his hair.		
She is cleaning the house.		
She is getting out of bed.		
He is getting undressed.		
He is eating dinner.		

Circle the picture that matches the sentence.

He is driving his car.		
He is at work.		
She is shopping for food.		
She is washing dishes.		
She is waking up.		
She is leaving the house.		

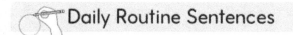

Circle the picture that matches the sentence.

She is having a snack.		
She is stretching.		
She is making dinner.		
He is taking a bath.		
She is doing her homework.		
He is riding his bike.		

Find the sentence that matches the picture.

He is eating breakfast. ◯		He is eating breakfast. ◯
He is brushing his hair. ◯		He is brushing his hair. ◯
She is making dinner. ◯		She is watching T.V. ◯

He is eating breakfast. ◯		He is reading a book. ◯
He is brushing his teeth. ◯		He is making his bed. ◯
She is making the bed. ◯		She is making dinner. ◯

He is eating breakfast. ◯		He is getting dressed. ◯
She is working out. ◯		She is brushing his hair. ◯
She is making dinner. ◯		She is eating lunch. ◯

She is getting dressed. ◯		He is eating breakfast. ◯
He is taking a bath. ◯		She is taking a shower. ◯
She is sleeping. ◯		She is brushing her hair. ◯

He is doing homework. ◯		He is eating breakfast. ◯
He is eating dinner. ◯		He is getting dressed. ◯
She is making her bed. ◯		She is making dinner. ◯

He is brushing his har. ◯		He is eating breakfast. ◯
He is doing his homework. ◯		He is brushing his hair. ◯
She is making dinner. ◯		He is washing his face. ◯

Find the sentence that matches the picture.

She is shopping for food. ◯	She is making dinner. ◯
He is brushing his hair. ◯	He is driving his car. ◯
He is doing laundry. ◯	He is watching T.V. ◯
He is eating breakfast. ◯	He is making dinner. ◯
He is at the store. ◯	He is at work. ◯
He is brushing his hair. ◯	She is doing laundry. ◯
He is eating breakfast. ◯	He is getting dressed. ◯
She is cleaning the house. ◯	She is shopping for food. ◯
She is making dinner. ◯	She is eating lunch. ◯
She is getting dressed. ◯	He is eating breakfast. ◯
She is getting out of bed. ◯	She is washing dishes. ◯
She is reading. ◯	She is brushing her hair. ◯
He is doing homework. ◯	She is waking up. ◯
He is eating dinner. ◯	He is getting dressed. ◯
He is getting undressed. ◯	She is making dinner. ◯
He is brushing his har. ◯	She is doing laundry. ◯
He is going to bed. ◯	He is brushing his hair. ◯
She is making dinner. ◯	She is leaving the house. ◯

Find the sentence that matches the picture.

	She is shopping for food. ◯	
	She is making her bed. ◯	
	He is getting dressed. ◯	

She is reading a book. ◯	
She is having a snack. ◯	
He is at work. ◯	

She is taking a shower. ◯	
She is washing the dishes. ◯	
He is brushing his hair. ◯	

He is making dinner. ◯	
She is stretching. ◯	
She is doing laundry. ◯	

He is eating breakfast. ◯	
She is cleaning the house. ◯	
He is putting on his pajamas. ◯	

She is making dinner. ◯	
She is cleaning the house. ◯	
He is getting dressed. ◯	

She is leaving for school. ◯	
She is getting out of bed. ◯	
She is reading. ◯	

He is eating breakfast. ◯	
He is taking a bath. ◯	
She is brushing her hair. ◯	

She is making dinner. ◯	
He is eating dinner. ◯	
She is reading her book. ◯	

She is waking up. ◯	
She is doing her homework. ◯	
She is making dinner. ◯	

They are getting on the bus. ◯	
They are eating lunch. ◯	
They are watching T.V. ◯	

He is riding his bike. ◯	
He is brushing his hair. ◯	
She is taking a bath. ◯	

Write the missing words in each sentence. Verbs (actions)

Nouns	
breakfast	book
homework	teeth

eating	sleeping
brushing	reading
working out	

He is _____ _____.
  verb   noun

He is _____ his

_____.
  verb   noun

She is _____ ____.
          verb

She is _____.
          verb

He is _____ a ____.
          verb   noun

He is doing his _____.
                      noun

Write the missing words in each sentence. Verbs (actions)

Nouns		
face	hair	T.V.
lunch	bed	

washing	watching
brushing	eating
getting dressed	

She is _____ _____.
_{verb}   _{noun}

He is going to ____.
_{noun}

She is _____ _____.
_{verb}   _{noun}

She is _____
_{verb}
her ____.
_{noun}

He is _____ _____.
_{verb}

He is _____ his _____.
_{verb}   _{noun}

Write the missing words in each sentence. Verbs (actions)

Nouns				cleaning	brushing
dinner	laundry			eating	
bed	hair			getting undressed	

She is doing _____.
_{noun}

He is _____ his ____.
_{verb}   _{noun}

She is _____ the house.
_{verb}

She is getting out of ___.
_{noun}

He is _____ _____.
_{verb}

He is _____ his _____.
_{verb}   _{noun}

Write the missing words in each sentence. Verbs (actions)

Nouns

food	car	work
house	dishes	

leaving	washing
driving	shopping
waking up	

He is _____ his ___.
  verb   noun

He is at ____.
  noun

She is _____ for
  verb
____.
noun

She is _____ _____.
  verb   noun

She is _____ ___.
  verb

She is _____
  verb
the ____.
  noun

Write the missing words in each sentence.

Nouns

bed	shower	bus
book	pajamas	

Verbs (actions)

reading	leaving

She is making her ____.
noun

She is taking a _____.
noun

He is putting on his _____.
noun

She is _____ for school.
verb

She is _____ her ____.
verb   noun

They are getting on the ____.
noun

Write the missing words in each sentence.

Nouns		
dinner	bath	bike
homework	snack	

Verbs (actions)	
riding	stretching

She is having a _____.
noun

She is _____.
verb

She is making _____.
noun

He is taking a _____.
noun

She is doing her _____.
noun

He is _____ his _____.
verb   noun

Write a sentence next to each picture.

Write a sentence next to each picture.

_____

_____

_____

_____

_____

_____

_____

_____

_____

_____

_____

_____

Write a sentence next to each picture.

Write a sentence next to each picture.

_____

_____

_____

_____

_____

_____

_____

_____

_____

_____

_____

_____

Write a sentence next to each picture.

Community

☆ Community Vocabulary

doctor	police officer	janitor	nurse
garbage collector	painter	crossing guard	bus driver
chef	farmer	plumber	cashier
hair stylist	electrician	lawyer	teacher
waiter	electrician	veterinarian	baker
firefighter	scientist	dentist	piolet

Community Workers

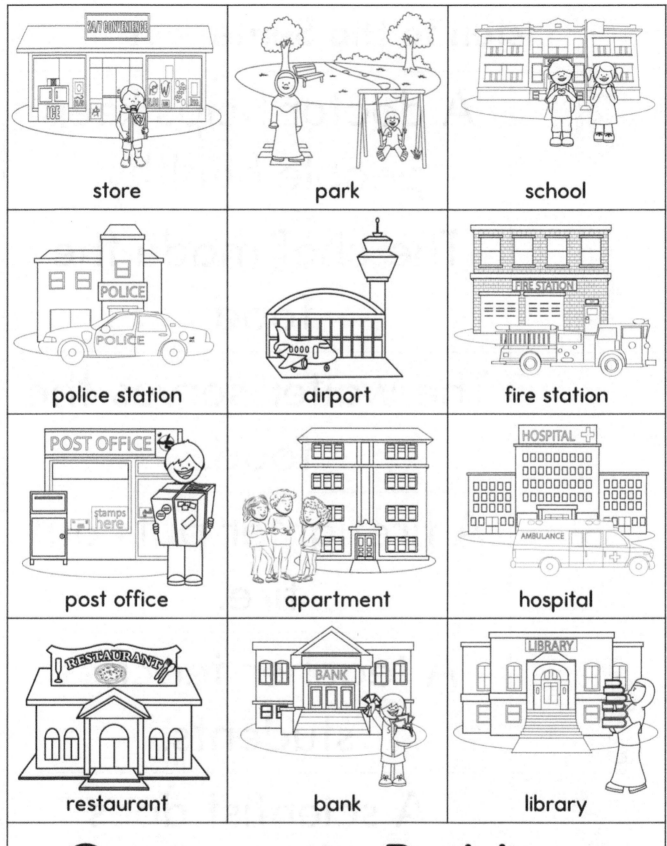

store

park

school

police station

airport

fire station

post office

apartment

hospital

restaurant

bank

library

Community Buildings

Listen to the Sentences

	A doctor helps keep people healthy.
	The chef made the food.
	The waiter serves the food.
	A firefighter puts out fire.
	A teacher teaches students.
	A scientist does experiments.

Listen to the Sentences

	This police officer keeps people safe.
	The farmer grows food.
	The nurse takes care of sick people.
	The cashier helps the shopper.
	The baker bakes a cake.
	The pilot flies the plane.

Listen to the Sentences

	A janitor helps keep a building clean.
	A plumber can fix a toilet.
	A veterinarian helps hurt animals.
	A dentist takes care of teeth.
	The bus driver drives a bus.
	The construction worker builds a house.

Listen to the Sentences

	The garbage collector takes away trash.
	A painter paints walls.
	The crossing guard helps people cross the road.
	The electrician fixes the lights.
	A lawyer helps people with the law.
	A hair stylist cuts hair.

Listen to the Sentences

	People shop in a store.
	The police car is at the police station.
	Bring a package to the post office.
	You can eat pizza at a restaurant.
	The students go to school.
	Kids play at the park.

Listen to the Sentences

	The airplane is at the airport.
	People live at the apartment.
	You can get money from the bank.
	A fire engine parks at the fire station.
	An ambulance goes to the hospital.
	You can get books from the library.

Circle the picture that matches the sentence.

A doctor helps keep people healthy.		
The chef made the food.		
The waiter serves the food.		
A firefighter puts out fire.		
A teacher teaches students.		
A scientist does experiments.		

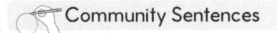

Circle the picture that matches the sentence.

This police officer keeps people safe.		
The farmer grows food.		
The nurse takes care of sick people.		
The cashier helps the shopper.		
The baker bakes a cake.		
The pilot flies the plane.		

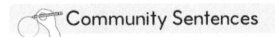

Circle the picture that matches the sentence.

A janitor helps keep a building clean.		
A plumber can fix a toilet.		
A veterinarian helps hurt animals.		
A dentist takes care of teeth.		
The bus driver drives a bus.		
The construction worker builds a house.		

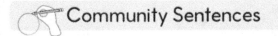

Circle the picture that matches the sentence.

Sentence	Picture 1	Picture 2
The garbage collector takes away trash.		
A painter paints walls.		
The crossing guard helps people cross the road.		
The electrician fixes the lights.		
A lawyer helps people with the law.		
A hair stylist cuts hair.		

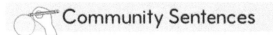
Circle the picture that matches the sentence.

People shop in a store.		
The police car is at the police station.		
Bring a package to the post office.		
You can eat pizza at a restaurant.		
The students go to school.		
Kids play at the park.		

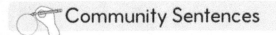
Circle the picture that matches the sentence.

The airplane is at the airport.		
People live at the apartment.		
You can get money from the bank.		
A fire engine parks at the fire station.		
An ambulance goes to the hospital.		
You can get books from the library.		

Find the sentence that matches the picture.

The doctor helps sick people. ○	This police officer keeps people safe. ○
The baker bakes a cake. ○	The firefighter puts out fires. ○
The cashier helps the shopper. ○	A chef makes food. ○
The teachers teaches students. ○	The cashier helps shoppers. ○
The nurse helps sick people. ○	The farmer grows food. ○
The chef made the food. ○	A teacher helps students. ○
The police help keep people safe. ○	A scientist does experiments. ○
The pilot flies a plane. ○	A baker can bake cake. ○
The waiter serves the food. ○	The nurse takes care of sick people. ○
A firefighter puts out fires. ○	A waiter brings out the food. ○
A chef cooks food. ○	A doctor helps keep people healthy. ○
A cashier rings up items. ○	A firefighter puts out fires. ○
A teacher teaches students. ○	The teacher helps students learn. ○
A pilot flies a plane. ○	The baker bakes a cake. ○
A farmer grows food. ○	She is making dinner. ○
A waiter serves food. ○	The baker bakes cake. ○
A firefighter puts out fires. ○	The nurse helps sick people. ○
A scientist does experiments. ○	The pilot flies the plane. ○

Find the sentence that matches the picture.

The doctor helps sick people. ○
The baker bakes a cake. ○
The garbage collector takes away trash. ○

A janitor helps keep a building clean. ○
The firefighter puts out fires. ○
A bus driver drives a bus. ○

A painter paints walls. ○
A janitor cleans up messes. ○
The chef made the food. ○

A crossing guard helps people cross the street. ○
A plumber can fix a toilet. ○
A teacher helps students. ○

The police help keep people safe. ○
The pilot flies a plane. ○
The crossing guard helps people cross the road. ○

A scientist does experiments. ○
A painter paints buildings. ○
A veterinarian helps hurt animals. ○

A firefighter puts out fires. ○
The electrician fixes the lights. ○
A cashier rings up items. ○

A construction worker builds houses. ○
A dentist takes care of teeth. ○
A firefighter puts out fires. ○

A crossing guard helps people cross the street. ○
A pilot flies a plane. ○
A lawyer helps people with the law. ○

The teacher helps students learn. ○
The baker bakes a cake. ○
The bus driver drives a bus. ○

A bus driver drives a bus. ○
A hair stylist cuts hair. ○
A scientist does experiments. ○

The baker bakes cake. ○
The construction worker builds a house. ○
The pilot flies the plane. ○

Find the sentence that matches the picture.

Picture	Sentences		Picture	Sentences	
	Mail a package at the post office.	◯		People live in an apartment.	◯
	You can get money at a bank.	◯		The airplane is at the airport.	◯
	People shop in a store.	◯		You can get money from the bank.	◯
	Sick people go to the hospital.	◯		You can get food from a restaurant.	◯
	People eat food at a restaurant.	◯		You can get a package from the post office.	◯
	The police car is at the police station.	◯		People live at the apartment.	◯
	An ambulance goes to the hospital.	◯		The police car is at the police station.	◯
	The students go to school.	◯		You can get money from the bank.	◯
	Bring a package to the post office.	◯		The nurse takes care of sick people.	◯
	You can get money at a bank.	◯		A fire engine parks at the fire station.	◯
	A fire engine stays at the fire station.	◯		People play at the park.	◯
	You can eat pizza at a restaurant.	◯		You can get food from a restaurant.	◯
	People live in an apartment.	◯		You can get a package from the post office.	◯
	The students go to school.	◯		People live in an apartment.	◯
	An ambulance goes to the hospital.	◯		An ambulance goes to the hospital.	◯
	People live in an apartment.	◯		A fire engine parks at the fire station.	◯
	You can get books from the library.	◯		You can get food from a restaurant.	◯
	Kids play at the park.	◯		You can get books from the library.	◯

Write the missing words in each sentence.

Job

waiter	firefighter	doctor	serves	healthy	fire
scientist	teacher	chef	students	food	experiments

A _____ helps keep people
job
_____ .

The _____ made the _____ .
job

The _____ _____ the food.
job

A _____ puts out
job
_____ .

A _____ teaches
job
_____ .

A _____ does
job
_____ .

Write the missing words in each sentence.

Job

piolet	nurse	cashier
farmer	police officer	baker

sick	plane	grows
shopper	safe	cake

The _____ _____ keeps
people ____.
        job

The _____ _____ food.
        job

The _____ takes care of
        job
____ people.

The _____ helps the
        job
_____ .

The _____ bakes a ____ .
        job

The _____ flies the ____ .
        job

Write the missing words in each sentence.

Job

garbage collector	painter	hair stylist		road	lights	trash
crossing guard	lawyer	electrician		law	hair	paints

The _____ _____
takes away _____.
_{job}

A _____ _____ walls.
_{job}

The _____ _____ helps
_{job}
people cross the _____.

The _____ fixes the
_{job}
_____.

A _____ helps people with the
_{job}
___.

A ____ _____ cuts _____.
_{job}

Content:

Community Missing Words

Write the missing words in each sentence.

Job

construction worker	janitor	veterinarian	drives	animals	house
bus driver	dentist	plumber	teeth	toilet	clean

A _____ helps keep a building _____.
(job)

The _____ can fix a _____.
(job)

The _____ _____ the food.
(job)

A _____ helps hurt _____.
(job)

The ___ _____ _____ a bus.
(job)

A _____ _____ a house.
(job)

© A World of Language Learners   59

Write the missing words in each sentence.

Location

restaurant	post office	park
school	police station	store

play	students	package
car	shop	eat

	People _____ in the _____. location
	A police ___ is at the _____ _____. location
	Bring a _____ to the _____ _____. location
	You can ___ pizza in a _____. location
	The _____ go to _____. location
	Kids _____ at the ___. location

Write the missing words in each sentence.

Location

hospital	library	apartment	books	airplane	ambulance
bank	airport	fire station	live	money	fire engine

The _____ is at the _____.
location

People _____ at the _____.
location

You can get _____ from the ____.
location

A _____ _____ parks at the _____ _____.
location

An _____ goes to the _____.
location

You can get _____ at the _____.
location

Write a sentence next to each picture.

Write a sentence next to each picture.

Write a sentence next to each picture.

Write a sentence next to each picture.

Write a sentence next to each picture.

Write a sentence next to each picture.

School

music teacher	art teacher	librarian
P.E. teacher	bus driver	cafeteria worker
secretary	crossing guard	janitor
principal	teacher	nurse

School Workers

library

lab

music room

bus

clinic

outside

office

closet

cafeteria

art room

gym

classroom

School Places

paper	scissors	clipboard
pen	pencil	crayons
sticky notes	backpack	headphones
highlighter	eraser	glue

School Supplies

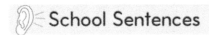

Listen to the Sentences

	The music teacher teaches us to play music.
	The P.E. teacher teaches me to stay fit.
	The secretary answers the phone.
	My teacher helps me learn.
	The nurse helps kids that get sick.
	The principal helps run the school.

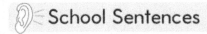

Listen to the Sentences

	The art teacher teaches us how to paint.
	The bus driver takes kids to school.
	The crossing guard stops the cars.
	The janitor helps keep the school clean.
	The librarian helps me find a good book.
	The cafeteria worker serves food.

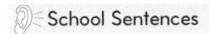

Listen to the Sentences

	The science teacher works in the science lab.
	The nurse works in the clinic.
	The janitor has a supply closet.
	The P.E. teacher works in the gym.
	The cafeteria worker works in the cafeteria.
	The teacher works in a classroom.

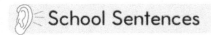

Listen to the Sentences

	The librarian works in the library.
	The bus driver drives a bus.
	The secretary works in the office.
	The art teacher works in the art room.
	The music teacher works in the music room.
	The crossing guard works outside.

Listen to the Sentences

	I can write on paper.
	I can use a pen to write.
	I can use sticky notes to write notes.
	I can use a highlighter to show important information.
	I can use a clipboard to hold paper.
	I can use crayons to draw.

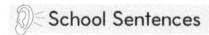

Listen to the Sentences

	I can use scissors to cut.
	I can use a pencil to write.
	I can put things in a backpack.
	I can use an eraser to fix a mistake.
	I listen with headphones.
	I can use glue to stick.

Circle the picture that matches the sentence.

The music teacher teaches us to play music.		
The P.E. teacher teaches me to stay fit.		
The secretary answers the phone.		
My teacher helps me learn.		
The nurse helps kids that get sick.		
The principal helps run the school.		

Circle the picture that matches the sentence.

The art teacher teaches us how to paint.		
The bus driver takes kids to school.		
The crossing guard stops the cars.		
The janitor helps keep the school clean.		
The librarian helps me find a good book.		
The cafeteria worker serves food.		

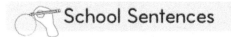 School Sentences

Circle the picture that matches the sentence.

The librarian works in the library.		
The bus driver drives a bus.		
The secretary works in the office.		
The art teacher works in the art room.		
The music teacher works in the music room.		
The crossing guard works outside.		

Circle the picture that matches the sentence.

The science teacher works in the science lab.		
The nurse works in the clinic.		
The janitor has a supply closet.		
The P.E. teacher works in the gym.		
The cafeteria worker works in the cafeteria.		
The teacher works in a classroom.		

Find the sentence that matches the picture.

	The art teacher teaches us how to paint.	○		This police officer keeps people safe.	○
	The music teacher teaches us to play music.	○		The music teacher teaches us to play music.	○
	The janitor helps keep the school clean.	○		The bus driver takes kids to school.	○
	My teacher helps me learn.	○		The librarian helps me find a good book.	○
	The bus driver takes kids to school.	○		The principal helps run the school.	○
	The secretary answers the phone.	○		The P.E. teacher teaches me to stay fit.	○
	The crossing guard stops the cars.	○		The crossing guard stops the cars.	○
	The P.E. teacher helps me to stay fit.	○		The secretary answers the phone.	○
	The art teacher teaches me to paint.	○		The librarian helps me find a good book.	○
	The nurse helps kids that get hurt.	○		The cafeteria worker serves food.	○
	The librarian helps me find a good book.	○		The janitor helps keep the school clean.	○
	The janitor helps keep the school clean.	○		My teacher helps me learn.	○
	The principal helps run the school.	○		The teacher helps students learn.	○
	The librarian helps me find a good book.	○		The nurse helps kids that get sick.	○
	The bus driver takes kids to school.	○		The art teacher teaches me to paint.	○
	The P.E. teacher helps me to stay fit.	○		The principal helps run the school.	○
	The crossing guard stops cars.	○		My teacher helps me learn.	○
	The cafeteria worker serves food.	○		The janitor helps keep the school clean.	○

Find the sentence that matches the picture.

	The nurse works in the clinic.	◯
	The bus driver drives a bus.	◯
	The principal has an office.	◯

	The music teacher works in the music room.	◯
	The librarian drives a bus.	◯
	The librarian works in the library.	◯

	The art teacher works in the art room.	◯
	The nurse works in the clinic.	◯
	The P.E. teacher works in the gym.	◯

	The bus driver works in the cafeteria.	◯
	The nurse works in the clinic.	◯
	The bus driver drives a bus.	◯

	The police help keep people safe.	◯
	The pilot flies a plane.	◯
	The janitor has a supply closet.	◯

	The secretary works in the cafeteria.	◯
	The P.E. teacher works in the gym.	◯
	The secretary works in the office.	◯

	The P.E. teacher works in the gym.	◯
	The secretary works in the office.	◯
	The P.E. teacher works in the music room.	◯

	The art teacher works on the street.	◯
	The cafeteria worker works in the music room.	◯
	The art teacher works in the art room.	◯

	The cafeteria worker works in the music room.	◯
	The bus driver drives a bus.	◯
	The cafeteria worker works in the cafeteria.	◯

	The nurse works in the clinic.	◯
	The music teacher works in a supply closet.	◯
	The music teacher works in the music room.	◯

	The teacher works in a classroom.	◯
	The crossing guard works on the street.	◯
	The music teacher works in the music room.	◯

	The crossing guard works in the art room.	◯
	The crossing guard works outside.	◯
	The secretary works in the office.	◯

Find the sentence that matches the picture.

I can use scissors to stick. ◯	I can use scissors to cut. ◯
I can use scissors to cut. ◯	I can use paper to hold things. ◯
I can use paper to write on. ◯	I can write on paper. ◯
I can use a pencil to write. ◯	I can use a pen to write. ◯
I can put things in a backpack. ◯	I can use scissors to cut. ◯
I can use a pencil to stick. ◯	I can use a pen to stick. ◯
I can use a backpack to write. ◯	I can use sticky notes to write notes. ◯
I can use scissors to cut. ◯	I can use sticky notes to hold things. ◯
I can put things in a backpack. ◯	I can use a clipboard to hold paper. ◯
I can use an eraser to fix a mistake. ◯	I can use a highlighter to cut. ◯
I can use a clipboard to hold paper. ◯	I can use glue to stick. ◯
I can use an eraser to stick. ◯	I can use a highlighter to show important information. ◯
I can use markers to hold things. ◯	I can use scissors to cut. ◯
I listen with headphones. ◯	I can use a clipboard to draw. ◯
I can use a clipboard to hold things. ◯	I can use a clipboard to hold paper. ◯
I can use glue to cut. ◯	I can put things in a backpack. ◯
I can use glue to stick. ◯	I can use crayons to cut. ◯
I can use a clipboard to hold paper. ◯	I can use crayons to draw. ◯

Write the missing words in each sentence.

Job

phone	stay fit
get sick	play music
learn	school

P.E teacher	nurse	secretary
teacher	music teacher	principal

The_____ _____ teaches
us to ____ _____.
_{job}

The_____ helps run the
_____.
_{job}

The _____ teaches me
to _____ ____.
_{job}

The _____ answers the
_____.
_{job}

My _____ helps me _____.
_{job}

The _____ helps kids that gets
_____.
_{job}

Write the missing words in each sentence.

Job			book	food
librarian	janitor	cafeteria worker	clean	school
art teacher	bus driver	crossing guard	paint	cars

The _____ _____ teaches us how to ^{job} _____.

The ___ _____ takes kids to _{job} _____.

The _____ _____ stops the ____. _{job}

The _____ helps keep the school ^{job} _____.

The _____ helps me find a good ^{job} _____.

The _____ _____ serves _____. _{job}

Write the missing words in each sentence.   Place

Job			Place	
			art room	outside
art teacher	librarian	crossing guard	library	office
bus driver	music teacher	secretary	bus	music room

The_____ works in the

job

_____.

place

The ___ _____drives the

job

___.

place

The _____ works in the

job

_____.

place

The ___ _____ works in

job

the ___ _____.

place

The _____ _____ works in

job

the _____ _____.

place

The _____ _____ works

job

_____.

place

Write the missing words in each sentence.

	Job			Place	
				cafeteria	lab
nurse	janitor	cafeteria worker		classroom	gym
teacher	P.E. teacher	science teacher		supply closet	clinic

The _____ _____ works in the science ___.

(job) (place)

The _____ works in the _____.

(job) (place)

The _____ has a _____ _____.

(job) (place)

The ___ _____ works in the ___.

(job) (place)

The _____ _____ works in the _____.

(job) (place)

The _____ works in the _____.

(job) (place)

Write the missing words in each sentence.

	Supply			important	write
highlighter	pen	sticky notes		hold	notes
clipboard	crayons	paper		write	draw

I can _____ on _____.
_{supply}

I can use a ___ to ____.
_{supply}

I can use _____ _____to write _____.
_{supply}

I can use a _____ to show _____ information.
_{supply}

I can use a _____ to ____ paper.
_{supply}

I can use _____ to ____.
_{supply}

Write the missing words in each sentence.

Supply

scissors	eraser	glue
backpack	pencil	headphones

cut	write
mistake	put things
stick	listen

	I can use _____ to ___. supply
	I can use a _____ to supply _____.
	I ____ _____ in a _____. supply
	I can use an _____ to fix a supply _____.
	I _____ with _____. supply
	I can use _____ to _____. supply

Write a sentence next to each picture.

Write a sentence next to each picture.

Write a sentence next to each picture.

Write a sentence next to each picture.

Write a sentence next to each picture.

_____

_____

_____

_____

_____

_____

_____

_____

_____

_____

_____

_____

Write a sentence next to each picture.

Terms of Use

Thank you for purchasing this product.
The contents are the property of Ellie Tiemann and licensed to you only for classroom/personal use as a single user. I retain the copyright, and reserve all rights to this product.

You may not claim this work as your own, giveaway, or sell any portion of this product. You may not share this product anywhere on the internet or on school share sites.

Find more teaching resources at

https://www.teacherspayteachers.com/Store/A-World-Of-Language-Learners

Get weekly tips and find out about teaching resources at

https://www.aworldoflanguagelearners.com/newsletter/

Made in the USA
Coppell, TX
17 October 2024

38752237R10057